MICHAEL JACKSON
Instrumental Solos

CONTENTS

Arranged by BILL GALLIFORD, ETHAN NEUBURG and TOD EDMONDSON

Produced by
Alfred Music Publishing Co., Inc.
P.O. Box 10003
Van Nuys, CA 91410-0003
alfred.com

Printed in USA.

ISBN-10: 0-7390-7803-8
ISBN-13: 978-0-7390-7803-7

Alfred Cares. Contents printed on 100% recycled paper.

BEAT IT

Written and Composed by
MICHAEL JACKSON

Moderately fast ♩ = 138

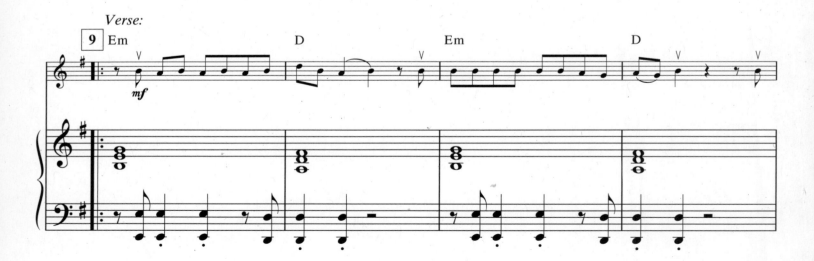

3

Chorus:

Beat It - 4 - 2

4

47 E5

D5

E5

D5

Em7

D5

E5

Beat It - 4 - 4

BILLIE JEAN

Written and Composed by
MICHAEL JACKSON

Billie Jean - 5 - 1

Chorus:

*E♯=F♮.

BLACK OR WHITE

Rap Lyrics Written by
BILL BOTTRELL

Written and Composed by
MICHAEL JACKSON

Black or White - 5 - 1

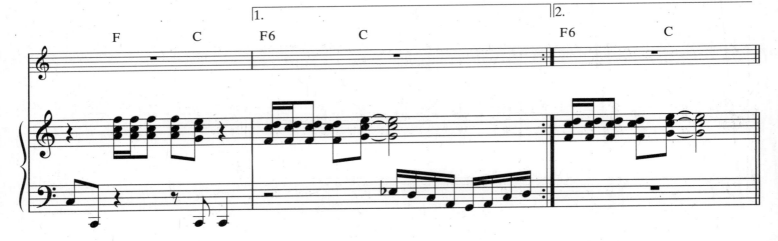

33 *Optional Rap:*

(Spoken:) Protection for gangs, clubs, and nations, causing grief in human relations.

It's a turf war, on a global scale. I'd rather hear both sides of the tale.

You see, it's not about races, just places,   faces. Where your blood comes from is where your space is.

I've seen the sharp get duller,   I'm not going to spend my life being a color.

15

Black or White - 5 - 5

DON'T STOP 'TIL YOU GET ENOUGH

Written and Composed by
MICHAEL JACKSON

Don't Stop 'til You Get Enough - 5 - 1

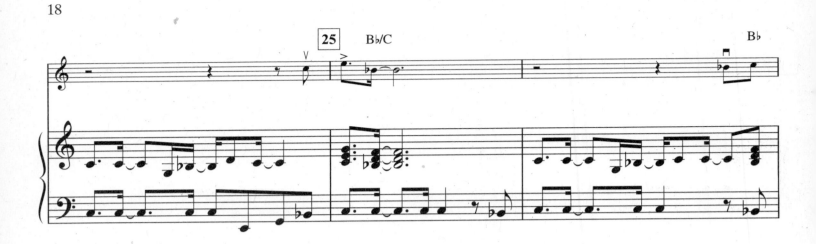

33 *Chorus:*

Chorus:

51 B♭maj7/C

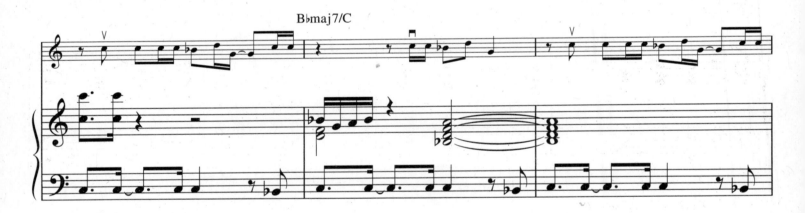

HUMAN NATURE

Words and Music by
JOHN BETTIS and JEFF PORCARO

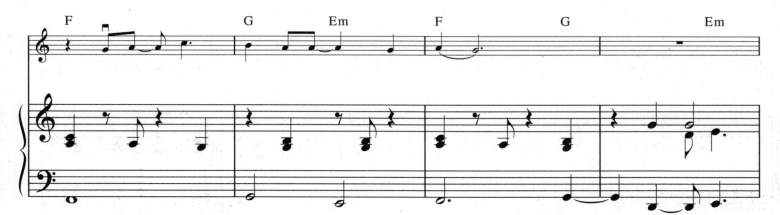

Human Nature - 5 - 1

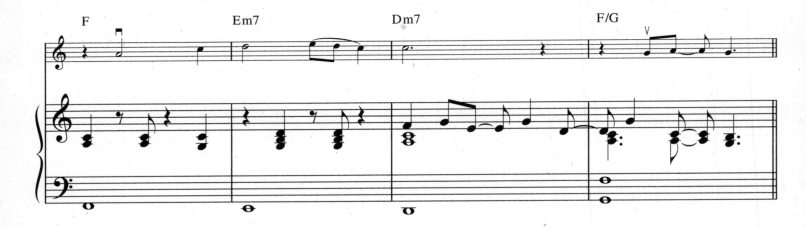

Human Nature - 5 - 3

D.S. 𝄉 *al Coda*

Human Nature - 5 - 5

I JUST CAN'T STOP LOVING YOU

Written and Composed by
MICHAEL JACKSON

I Just Can't Stop Loving You - 4 - 1

I Just Can't Stop Loving You - 4 - 3

Alfred's
INSTRUMENTAL PLAY-ALONG

MICHAEL JACKSON
Instrumental Solos

Arranged by BILL GALLIFORD, ETHAN NEUBURG and TOD EDMONDSON

Alfred

Produced by
Alfred Music Publishing Co., Inc.
P.O. Box 10003
Van Nuys, CA 91410-0003
alfred.com

Printed in USA.

ISBN-10: 0-7390-7803-8
ISBN-13: 978-0-7390-7803-7

CONTENTS

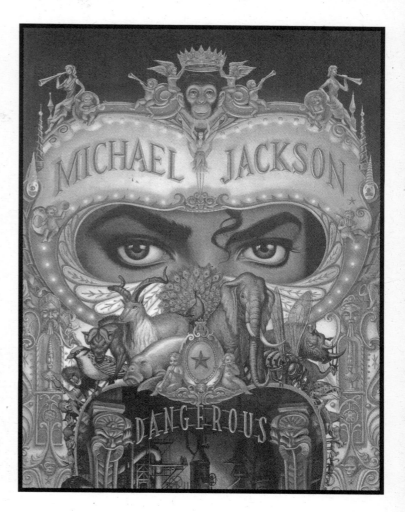

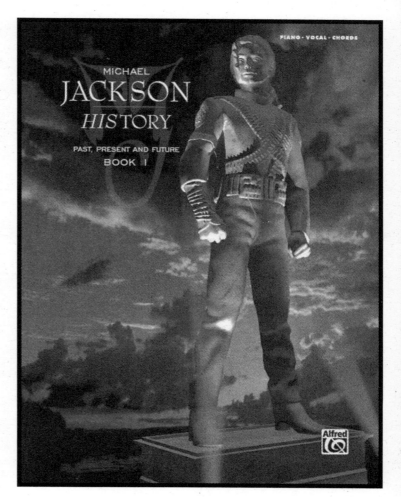

BEAT IT

Track 2: Demo
Track 3: Play Along

Written and Composed by
MICHAEL JACKSON

Beat It - 2 - 1

BILLIE JEAN

Track 4: Demo
Track 5: Play Along

Written and Composed by
MICHAEL JACKSON

*E♯=F♮.

Billie Jean - 2 - 1

37 *Chorus:*

51

BLACK OR WHITE

Rap Lyrics Written by
BILL BOTTRELL

Written and Composed by
MICHAEL JACKSON

Track 6: Demo
Track 7: Play Along

33 *Optional Rap:*

(Spoken:) Protection for gangs, clubs, and nations,   *causing grief in human relations.*

Black or White - 2 - 1

It's a turf war,   on a global scale.   I'd rather hear both sides of the tale.

You see, it's not about races, just places,   faces. Where your blood comes from is where your space is.

I've seen the sharp get duller,   I'm not going to spend my life being a color.

DON'T STOP 'TIL YOU GET ENOUGH

Track 8: Demo
Track 9: Play Along

Written and Composed by
MICHAEL JACKSON

Don't Stop 'til You Get Enough - 2 - 1

33 *Chorus:*

1.   2.

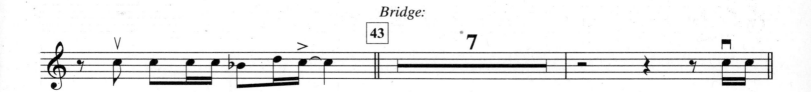

Bridge:

43   **7**

Chorus:

51

1.   2.

HUMAN NATURE

Track 10: Demo
Track 11: Play Along

Words and Music by
JOHN BETTIS and JEFF PORCARO

Human Nature - 2 - 1

I JUST CAN'T STOP LOVING YOU

Track 12: Demo
Track 13: Play Along

Written and Composed by
MICHAEL JACKSON

I Just Can't Stop Loving You - 2 - 1

Chorus:

I Just Can't Stop Loving You - 2 - 2

THE WAY YOU MAKE ME FEEL

Track 14: Demo
Track 15: Play Along

Written and Composed by
MICHAEL JACKSON

The Way You Make Me Feel - 2 - 1

To Coda ⊕

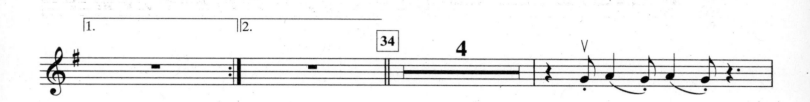

D.S. 𝄋 al Coda

⊕ *Coda*

The Way You Make Me Feel - 2 - 2

SHE'S OUT OF MY LIFE

Track 16: Demo
Track 17: Play Along

Words and Music by
TOM BAHLER

She's Out of My Life - 2 - 1

She's Out of My Life - 2 - 2

Track 18: Demo
Track 19: Play Along

WILL YOU BE THERE

Written and Composed by
MICHAEL JACKSON

Will You Be There - 2 - 1

Will You Be There - 2 - 2

MAN IN THE MIRROR

Words and Music by
SIEDAH GARRETT and GLEN BALLARD

Track 20: Demo
Track 21: Play Along

Moderately (♩ = 100)

Man in the Mirror - 2 - 1

Chorus:

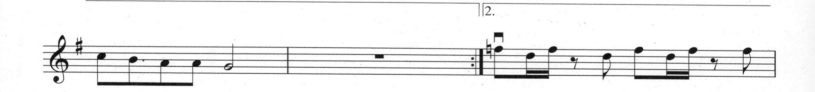

Man in the Mirror - 2 - 2

THRILLER

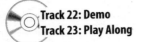

Track 22: Demo
Track 23: Play Along

Words and Music by
ROD TEMPERTON

Thriller - 2 - 1

YOU ARE NOT ALONE

Track 24: Demo
Track 25: Play Along

Words and Music by
R. KELLY

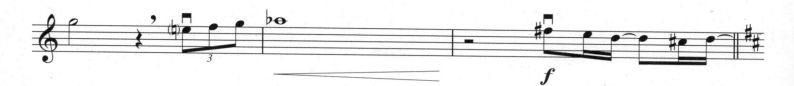

MICHAEL JACKSON
Instrumental Solos

BEAT IT

THE WAY YOU MAKE ME FEEL

BILLIE JEAN

SHE'S OUT OF MY LIFE

BLACK OR WHITE

WILL YOU BE THERE
(THEME FROM "FREE WILLY")

DON'T STOP 'TIL
YOU GET ENOUGH

MAN IN THE MIRROR

HUMAN NATURE

THRILLER

I JUST CAN'T STOP LOVING YOU

YOU ARE NOT ALONE

This book is part of a string series arranged for Violin, Viola, and Cello. The arrangements are completely compatible with each other and can be played together or as solos. Each book features a specially designed piano accompaniment that can be easily played by a teacher or intermediate piano student, as well as a carefully crafted removable part, complete with bowings, articulations and keys well suited for the Level 2-3 player. A fully orchestrated accompaniment CD is also provided. The CD includes a DEMO track of each song, which features a live string performance, followed by a PLAY-ALONG track.

This book is also part of **Alfred's Michael Jackson Instrumental Solos** series written for Flute, Clarinet, Alto Sax, Tenor Sax, Trumpet, Horn in F and Trombone. An orchestrated accompaniment CD is included. A **piano accompaniment** book (optional) is also available. Due to level considerations regarding keys and instrument ranges, the arrangements in the **wind instrument** series are not compatible with those in the **string instrument** series.

Alfred

alfred.com

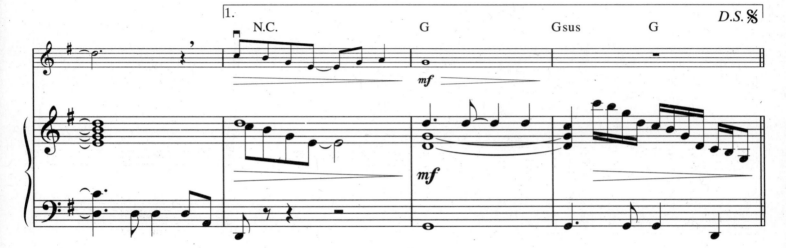

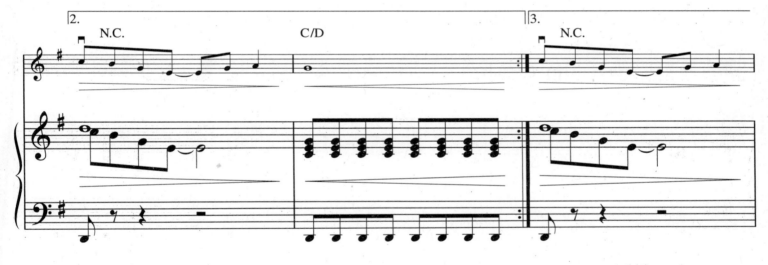

I Just Can't Stop Loving You - 4 - 4

THE WAY YOU MAKE ME FEEL

Written and Composed by
MICHAEL JACKSON

The Way You Make Me Feel - 5 - 1

Verse:

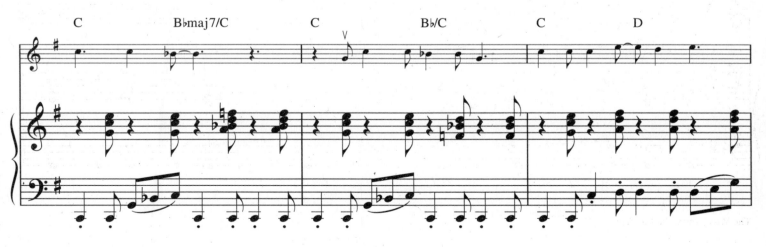

Chorus:

SHE'S OUT OF MY LIFE

Words and Music by
TOM BAHLER

She's Out of My Life - 3 - 1

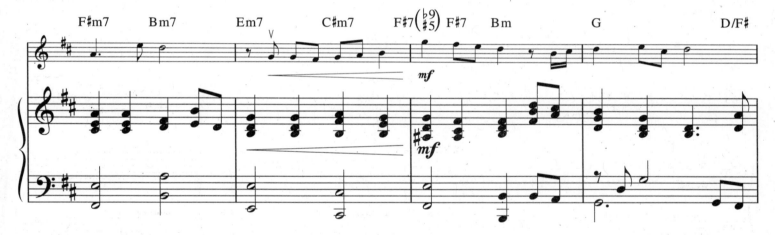

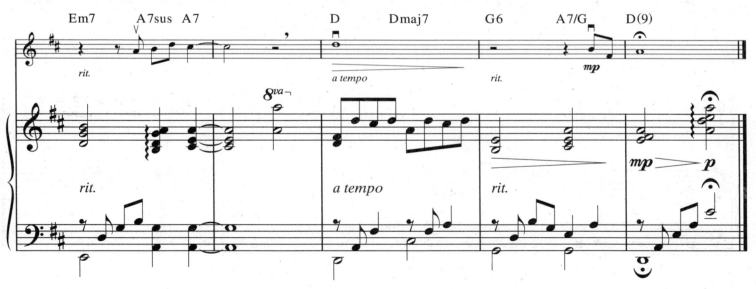

She's Out of My Life - 3 - 3

WILL YOU BE THERE

Written and Composed by
MICHAEL JACKSON

Moderate gospel feel (♩ = 80)

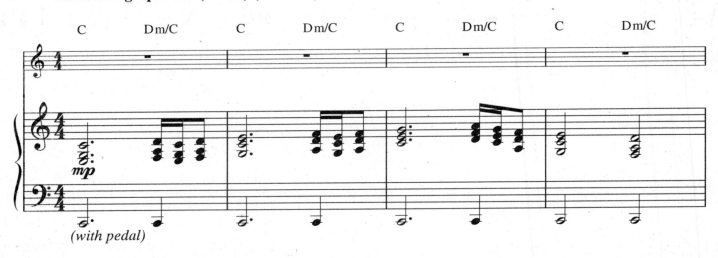

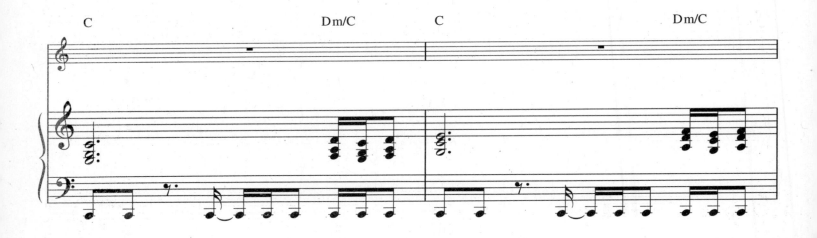

Will You Be There - 5 - 1

Bridge:

Verse:

42

Will You Be There - 5 - 5

MAN IN THE MIRROR

**Words and Music by
SIEDAH GARRETT and GLEN BALLARD**

Man in the Mirror - 3 - 1

Man in the Mirror - 3 - 3

THRILLER

Words and Music by
ROD TEMPERTON

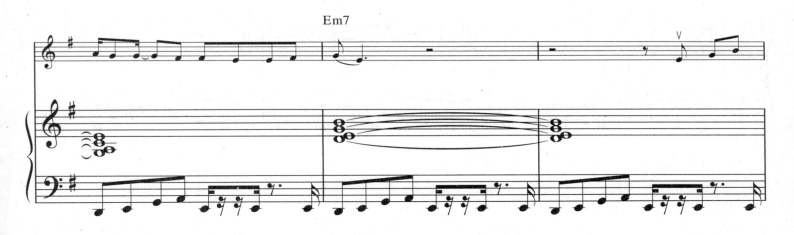

Thriller - 5 - 2

48

Thriller - 5 - 3

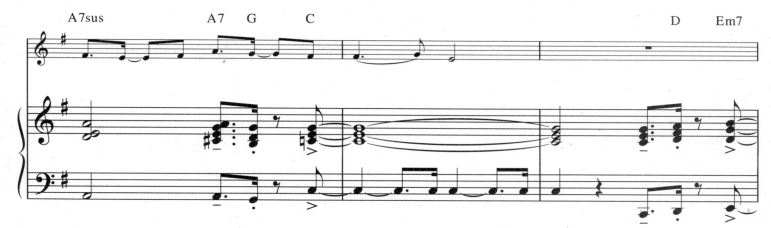

D.S. %% al Coda

YOU ARE NOT ALONE

Words and Music by
R. KELLY

Slowly ♩ = 60

Verse:

(with pedal)

You Are Not Alone - 5 - 1

52

You Are Not Alone - 5 - 3

54

Chorus:

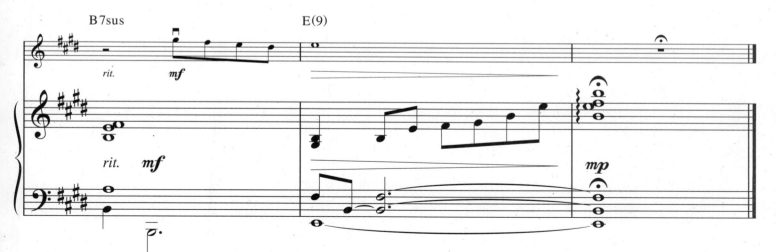

You Are Not Alone - 5 - 5

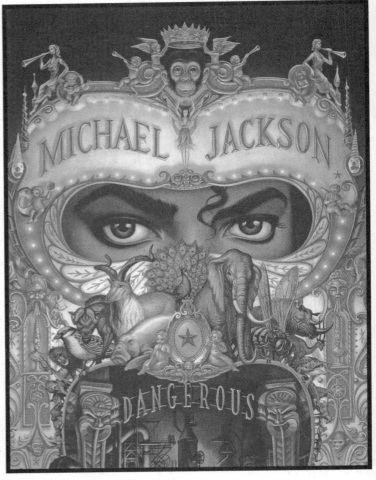

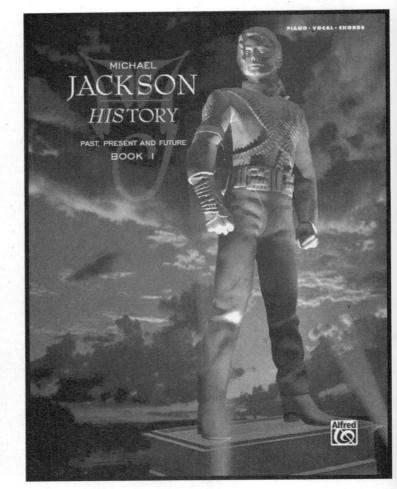